The many meeeees of

Miniki

Published in Australia by
Zen Publishing
156 Alexandra Parade, Alexandra Headland, Queensland, Australia
virginia@virginiarobin.com
www.virginiarobin.com.au

First published in Australia in 2024
Copyright © Virginia Robin 2024

National Library of Australia Cataloguing in Publication entry

A catalogue record for this book is available from the National Library of Australia

ISBN: 978-1-7635811-3-5 (paperback)
ISBN: 978-1-7635811-1-1 (hardback)
ISBN: 978-1-7635811-2-8 (epub)

Written and illustrated by Virginia Robin.

Printed by Kindle Direct Publishing

The many meeeees of
Miniki

Written and illustrated by
Virginia Robin

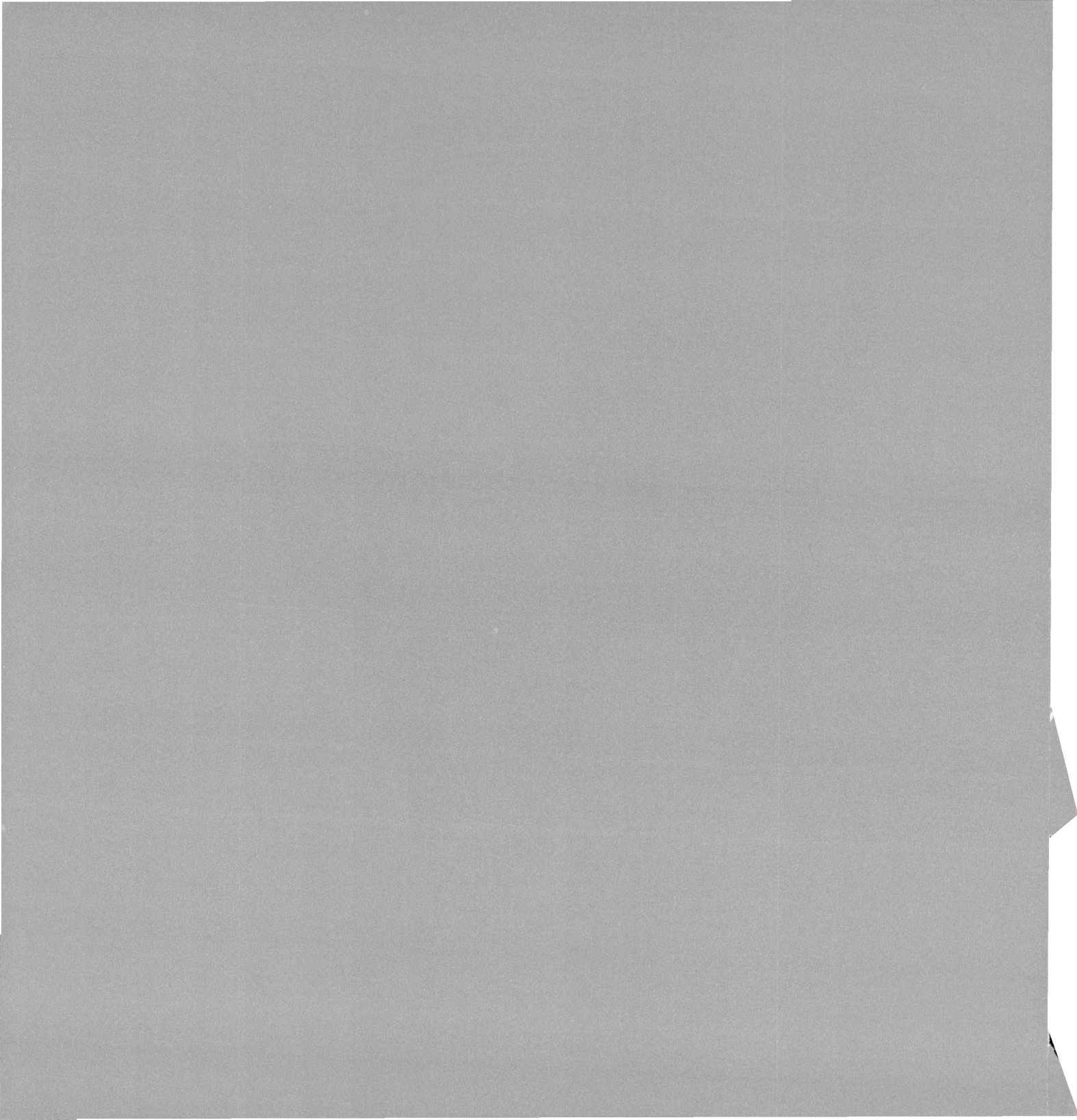

This book is dedicated
to Miniki's
very special
friends.

Suki   Ikki   Elaine Jerry

This is me.
Miniki.
There's more to me
than you can see.

This is me when I feel

LOVE

Inside me feels all cozy and warm.
This part of me helps friendships form.

What does love feel like to you?

This is me when I feel

SAD.

Inside me feels so heavy and blue,
which helps my little tears push through.

What does sad feel like to you?

This is me when I feel

CONFUSED

Inside me feels swirly and muddy
because I don't know what to choose.
This helps me listen to my heart
- it knows just what to do!

What does confused feel like to you?

This is me when I feel

HAPPY

Inside me feels quite light and free,
as I bounce all about with sunshiny glee.

What does happy feel like to you?

This is me when I feel

SCARED

Inside me feels jaggedy and cold.
It's quite okay I don't feel bold.

What does scared feel like to you?

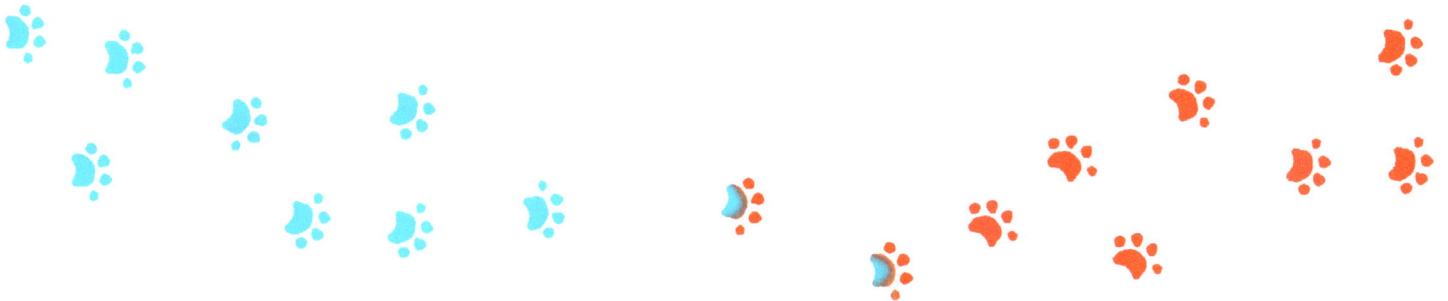

This is me when I feel

ANGRY

Inside me feels all hot and red.
This part tells me to say 'No!' instead.

What does angry feel like to you?

This is me when I feel

BRAVE

Inside me feels like a mighty tiger,
though I'm a little scared.
This part helps me feel so strong,
as though I am prepared.

What does brave feel like to you?

This is me when I feel like a

SUPERSTAR

Inside me feels way bigger than the sky.
This helps me feel confident as I learn to fly.

What does a superstar feel like to you?

This is me when I feel

MEH

Inside me feels all flat and dull.
I'm not quite at my best.
This part reminds me to take my time,
or to simply take a rest.

What does meh feel like to you?

This is me when I feel

GREEDY

Inside me feels hungry like nothing is enough.
I can want what I want, but just not too much.

What does greedy feel like to you?

This is me when I feel

SILLY

Inside me feels giggly and loud
and brightly coloured.
This part reminds me not to be
too serious or too bothered.

What does silly feel like to you?

This is me when I feel

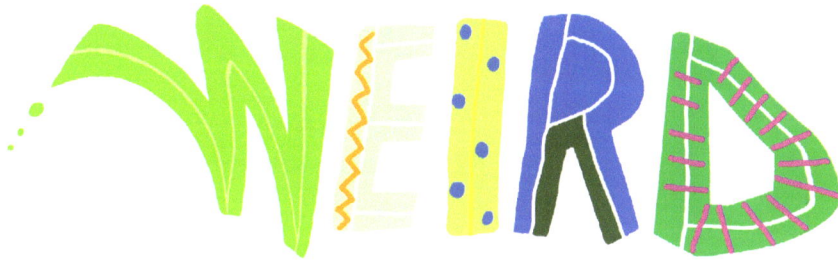

WEIRD

Inside me feels different,
in a kooky kind of way.
This reminds me that I am unique,
and creative every day.

What does weird feel like to you?

This is me when I feel

C

Inside me feels all light and airy,
like a fluffy cloud.
Most of the time, in my day,
I want this part around.

What does calm feel like to you?

All of my parts make me
the complete me ... ow.

Which part
of you
are you
feeling
right now?

www.ingramcontent.com/pod-product-compliance
Lightning Source LLC
LaVergne TN
LVHW072057070426
835508LV00002B/140